THE LOVE

*"The Child Who Received Recognition From
President Obama and Harvard University"*

SOBORNO ISAAC BARI

authorHOUSE®

AuthorHouse™
1663 Liberty Drive
Bloomington, IN 47403
www.authorhouse.com
Phone: 1 (800) 839-8640

Published by AuthorHouse 03/13/2019

ISBN: 978-1-7283-0196-9 (sc)
ISBN: 978-1-7283-0195-2 (e)

A Muslim woman joined the anti-terrorism movement: Farjana Marjia, a student of Jahangirnagar University, is the first woman to join the anti-terrorism revolution to help Soborno Isaac create a world without terrorism. By doing so, she has become the face of the anti-terrorism revolution and the Rosa Parks of all Bengali women. She was inspired by Isaac's movie and motivated to promote his message that we are all "Muslim, but we love all other religions, including Hinduism, Buddhism, Christianity, and a Judaism. We celebrate Eid, but we also love celebrating Christmas and other holidays."

Sadiyan Lima, a student of Dhaka University, is the second woman who joined Soborno Isaac to create a world without terrorism. By doing so, she has become the symbol of all Muslim women. As a response to this, I wrote a letter to my biographer, Dear Zahid, indicating that I wanted him to carry Sadiyan's poster to every village in Bangladesh to promote women's support for the fight against terrorism.

CONTENTS

DEDICATION

To President Obama

It was November 2016. A four-year-old boy with the weird name Soborno became famous around the world overnight after receiving recognition from President Obama for being able to solve PhD-level math, physics, and chemistry problems. This was followed by many other recognitions from renowned universities, such as Harvard. The boy decided to use his fame to launch *The Love,* a campaign to defeat terrorism by inspiring young people to fall in love with math and science.

I am this boy, and I want you to read my book and join my campaign *The Love.*

INTRODUCTION

I am pleased to write this forward for Soborno Issac's book "The Love." It is refreshing to know that in the world we live in today a child can conceptualize the meaning of love and how it can bring all of us together.

In a world where we try to differentiate from one another based on religion, race, and creed, it is important that we recognize that the most humanizing way to live on this earth is together through love and appreciating one another.

Soborno illustrated in his book how love can solve all problems. Love allows us to recognize our humanity and acknowledge that we all have a responsibility to one another, to create a better world for the generations coming after.

It is my wish that we embrace this principal to the fullest in the hopes of establishing a more peaceful and unified world. We can accomplish more together than we can apart.

Thomas A. Isekenegbe, Ph.D.
President
Bronx C. College

CHAPTER 1

ASKING THE IMAM TO PRAY FOR AMERICA

On April 9, 2012, I was born into a family that included a member who was a 9/11 survivor. On my second birthday, my father took me to 1 Liberty Plaza, where he worked as a security guard from 2001 to 2014. That day, he recollected the events of the most tragic morning in American history.

It was September 11, 2001. My father was working at the CUNY LaGuardia Community College Bookstore when terrorists attacked the Twin Towers. My uncle worked in the South Tower (World Trade Center [WTC] II). My dad ran to the WTC like a madman, managing to arrive downtown in 20 minutes. However, he was caught in the fallout of the first collapse (North Tower) as he ran toward the South Tower to find my uncle. My dad couldn't outrun the smoke and crawled under a van to avoid the debris. The air had turned black. He started choking, and his eyes burned. He thought the van that he was under would move and kill him. Someone dragged him into the van, and he later found himself in the hospital. In a panic, he fled the hospital and ran toward the Twin Towers again, with the hope of seeing my uncle, his younger brother.

Along with thousands of other terrified people, my father headed north on the West Side Highway. He waited there all day, watching all the events unfold, including the collapse of the South Tower, but he did not see his brother. He saw men and women jumping from windows in a desperate bid to escape the fire within the building. He saw them hit the ground and saw their blood on the street. He never forgot all these horrors (although, miraculously, his brother survived). Somehow, that story instilled a sense of patriotism in my blood. This patriotism gave me the audacity to ask my dad a question on July 3, 2016, when I was only four years old.

The day began with my dad and me going to the mosque. As we entered the public park, where the prayer was being held, I felt jolly and was ready to celebrate the Fourth of July. All of a sudden, I asked, "Dad, can I ask Imam to pray for America?" He didn't expect me to ask such question, because I was so young. Surprised, he looked at me and said reluctantly, "Go ahead." He thought that I would not have the audacity to do such a thing in front of hundreds of people at the mosque. But he was wrong.

(In the middle of the prayer, five-year-old Soborno Isaac suddenly stood up and shouted, "Excuse me, Imam! Can you please pray for my country, the United States of America, because tomorrow is the Fourth of July?" Unexpectedly, the imam ignored him, and Soborno sat back down.)

In the middle of the prayer, I stood up, and shouted, "Excuse me, Imam! Can you please pray for my country, the United States of America, because tomorrow is the Fourth of July?" As expected, the imam ignored me, and I sat back down.

On my way home, I was very sad and wouldn't talk. My dad asked me why I was so sad, and I said, "Dad, why didn't the imam pray for my country in his monazat?"

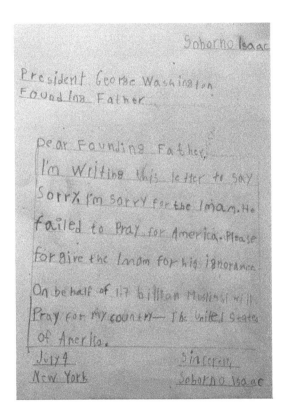

**(When the imam refused to pray for America, Soborno Isaac
decided to write an apology letter to the founding father:
"I think George Washington deserves an apology from
the imam. But since the imam will never apologize, I will
apologize on behalf of the imam and 1.8 billion Muslims.")**

"Forgive the imam," my dad said.

After we arrived at home, Dad wanted me to solve some problems with him. However, he realized that my mind was elsewhere. So, he asked me, "Why aren't you paying attention?"

Once again, my response shocked him: "Dad, I want to write a letter to George Washington."

"Why?"

"I think the founding father deserves an apology from the imam. But since the imam will never apologize, I will apologize on behalf of the imam and 1.7 billion Muslims."

This time, my dad knew exactly what I was talking about. So, he let me go ahead.

I started writing a letter to George Washington, the founding father. When I showed the letter to my dad, he was shocked. He wrote in his diary, "How could a four-year-old have the understanding and the mental capability to not only address the wrongs of a religious preacher to a founding father but to also try to change it by asking the imam to pray for the US—something many adults would not dare to do?" And then, it dawned on my dad.

I told Dad that 10 events motivated me to rise against the imam's ignorance and launch a campaign against terrorism. In this book, I will share these 10 stories with you.

CHAPTER 2

TERROR AT NEW YORK UNIVERSITY

On December 16, 2014, I sat in sitting in the Bobst Library at New York University (NYU), solving some mathematics problems in preparation for my upcoming interview with Vice President Jerald Posman of Medgar Evers College. Suddenly, I heard my dad shouting at everyone in the library, "A new kind of war has been declared in the world's second-largest Muslim nation; it's a war against children." All the students gathered around the TV.

In the basement was a small cafeteria behind the student lounges, in which a large LCD TV monitor hung on the wall. As I passed by the television to head to the water fountain, I glanced upward at the TV and then turned away quickly.

Vice President Posman interviews me at CUNY Medgar Evers College

Faster than words can convey, I thought, *I believe I just saw terrorists killing schoolchildren!* I could scarcely believe my own eyes. I managed to drag myself to the nearest sofa, where my dad was sitting, and I faced the screen once more.

Then, I saw more blood—the blood of children.

Seven terrorists bearing AK-47s and rocket launchers moved toward the auditorium at the center of the school and opened fire indiscriminately on the children who had gathered there to sit an examination.

Tahira Kazi, the principal of the school, made an attempt to save the students, including five-year-old Khola Altaf. It had been Khola's second day of school. The Taliban disapproved of the principal's action, and Khola and other schoolchildren were forced to watch their teachers, including Kazi, being burned alive. Little Khola could take no more, and she and some other children ran toward the two exits on the other side of the auditorium as the terrorists opened fire. Many of the students were gunned down as they ran, including Khola, who was shot in the head.

At 9:30 p.m., my dad and I left NYU for home, believing that in a few days, I would think that I had not seen any of this on television. There is no benefit in being able to recall these events . . . no benefit in being able to remember the face of five-year-old Khola all covered in blood. There is no benefit in being able to remember the tiny coffins on the shoulders of parents. There is no benefit in remembering the blood of young children. So, I tried my best to forget everything I had seen. I thought that I would soon forget everything and would focus on my upcoming interview with Vice President Posman at Medgar Evers College.

However, I was wrong. I got home at around 10 p.m., and the memories all flooded back when my mom kissed me on the check. The following question popped into my head immediately: *what would Khola's mother do now?*

That night, I skipped dinner and hoped for a sound night's sleep that would help me forget the innocent faces of 130 dead children—especially Khola's. However, it all flooded back again in the morning as Dad dropped me off at school. *What would Khola's dad do now? Whom will he drop at school now?* For a moment, I felt as if I was the little brother of all 130 children who had been killed by the Taliban.

I decided to go to NYU, not to prepare for my interview with Vice President Posman but, rather, to take to the streets.

Over the next few days, my dad; my elder brother, Refath Bari; and I stood in front of the Bobst Library holding a banner that said, "The Taliban unleashed its terror again. This time, they decided to kill the angels—our children."

(My dad, who is a CRISP Scholar at NYU, demonstrates anti-terrorism campaign in front of NYU Bobst Library).

A few years ago, my dad founded the Bari Science Lab in Washington Square Park, the famous NYU campus, to create a campaign against the IS. The Bari Science Lab is based on a simple motto that is geared toward every single child: "Let's fall in love with math and science." Once we accomplish our goal, there will be no terrorism, because people will be too busy solving problems instead of creating them. So, I ask every one of the 1.6 billion Muslims worldwide to join our campaign. Let's fall in love with math and science!

CHAPTER 3

TERROR IN WASHINGTON

I love French, but I've never been a fan of *Charlie Hebdo*, the French satirical newspaper that published a series of cartoons of the Prophet Muhammad. But I switched my position during my brief visit to the Voice of America (VOA) building in Washington, D.C., on January 7, 2015.My dad and I left New York for D.C. at 5:00 a.m. I was scheduled to be interviewed by VOA at 11:00 a.m., but we arrived in the capital some 30 minutes late. My heart raced as my dad parked his car in front of the Smithsonian Museum.

Wondering whether Sabrina Dona would still be waiting for us, my dad ran toward the VOA elevator, carrying me on his shoulders. The security officers stopped us and asked us to go through the metal detector. As we were complying with this request, I noticed that many of the guards were staring at us. Then, when they were searching my body, I realized that something was wrong.

(Subrina interviews me at VOA Office in Washington D.C. I was only 2 years-old then).

My eyes turned to a TV monitor that was on the wall adjacent to the metal detector. I saw two terrorists, brothers Said and Cherif Kouachi, armed with AK-47s, forcing their way into the *Charlie Hebdo* building. I had seen a similar incident on December 16 while at the NYU Library: seven terrorists had entered a Pakistan army school and killed over 130 schoolchildren, including five-year-old Khola. My whole body quivered, and my heart dropped; I hoped with all my heart that the perpetrators were not Muslims this time. After all, I am a Muslim. However, not 10 seconds later, I heard "Allahu Akbar!" and my heart broke into a million pieces.

The security guard, who was still searching my dad, looked at him and asked, "What does that mean?"

Dad explained, "'Allahu Akbar' used to mean 'God is great.' However, today it means violence, blood, and terrorism. It means 'I'm about to fire a rocket from Gaza to Israel to kill innocent people.' It means 'I'm about to use hijacked planes to fly into the Twin Towers.' It means 'I'm about to kill hundreds of schoolchildren.' It means 'I'm about to kill journalists.'

The Kouachi brothers proved my dad right. They started shooting while shouting "Allahu Akbar!" and they killed nine journalists who were attending a meeting, as well as Ahmed Merabet, a Muslim police officer. When I saw them shooting innocent people, I cried out loud, and tears trickled from my disbelieving eyes. I thought, *Kouachi brothers, you are not Muslims. You are not human beings. You are animals. You are disgusting bastards!*

(Engineer Golam Mowla and MIT Professor Mizanul Chowdhury, who writes codes for NASA International Space Station, interviews me at FOBANA, in front of thousands of people including Congresswoman Barbara Comstock).

On my way back to New York later that day, I kept asking my dad one question: What lesson did the brothers hope to teach France by killing its journalists? What was it that they hoped the French would learn from this terrorism? How could they kill journalists for making jokes about the Prophet Muhammad? Dad became emotional:

"Kouachi brothers, you killed journalists to make Allah happy? You just made him look bad.

You killed them to make the Prophet happy? You made him look worse.

You killed them to force France to respect Islam? You just killed 1.8 billion Muslims.

You wanted to kill freedom of speech? You made me into *Charlie Hebdo*.

Yes, now I'm *Charlie Hebdo*, although I was once its critic"

I asked my dad, "Do *Charlie Hebdo* cartoons present the truth about the Prophet?

"No."

"Should we be angry?"

"Absolutely not."

Peaceful Muslims should understand that so-called jihadists unleashed a terrible evil against Islam by killing the *Charlie Hebdo* journalists, Jewish shoppers, and French police. Hence, Muslims should unite to identify the growing jihadist tumor and to unleash education as a means of eradicating this tumor. If they unite, maybe they can convince the bad Muslims, especially those who have been raised to be religious fanatics, to understand that there is more to life than religion—mathematics and science, for example. The exhortation of Abdus Salam, famous Muslim Nobel Laureate, is appropriate here: Good Muslims of the world, let's unite to unleash education to defeat the Muslim terrorists before it is too late.

CHAPTER 4

I'M MUSLIM, AND I LOVE GAYS

Every morning since December 16, 2014, I have woken up in fear of another nightmare. On June 12, my fear reached the point where I could no longer watch the morning news on television.

That day, my dad woke me. We thought of celebrating Father's Day early at Hotel Marriott, but my parents have never been fans of hotels nor clubs. Instead, my dad took me to Lehman College, where I was expected to solve math problems prior to my interview on differential calculus with Dr. Ricardo Fernandez, the president of the college.

(Lehman College President Fernandez interviews me)

The security officers at the college, who were familiar to us because of our many visits, stopped us and asked where we wanted to go. I was surprised, because the same guards had helped me on many previous occasions. So, I assumed that they wanted to know which classroom needed to be opened. But instead, they interrogated us. My dad reminded the officers that a banner with his picture was hanging on the campus. But they insisted that the questions were mandatory, and we complied.

I noticed that the other officers, who were inside the security booth, were staring at us. When the guards started patting Dad down, I realized that something was wrong. On a TV monitor in the security booth, I saw a man, whom I now know was Omar Mateen. He was armed with a semi-automatic assault rifle and was indiscriminately shooting everyone in the packed Pulse nightclub, Florida.

I had watched a similar incident on television on December 16, when seven terrorists killed more than 130 children at a Pakistan army school. My heart dropped, and my body quivered. I hoped that Mateen would not be Muslim. But a few seconds later, I heard Mateen shout, "Allahu Akbar!" and I struggled to stop my tears.

As I watched Mateen shooting innocent people, my dad whispered, "Omar Mateen, you are not Muslim. You are not a human being. You are an animal. You are a disgusting bastard."

(Our campaign for LGBT equality)

I am a Muslim, and I love the LGBT community. I love all human beings of all religions, ethnicities, and cultures. I am not only a Muslim but also a Hindu, Buddhist, Jew, and Christian.

That day, we solved no math problems at the college. On our way home, I wondered what Mateen hoped to teach the US by killing innocent people. He may have tried to trick the American people into believing that he represented more than a billion Muslims. But President Obama was right when he said, "Groups like [the IS] . . . (falsely) claim that they are the true leaders of over a billion of Muslims around the world who reject their crazy notions."

After the horrific shooting at Pulse, one question become obvious: How can we prevent similar domestic terrorist acts in the future? How could Mateen, whom the FBI interviewed twice, buy two assault rifles? There is something deeply wrong with our laws, which allowed this crime to be committed. Incidents such as the Pulse massacre occur because lawmakers hesitate to restrict gun ownership. Buying guns is as easy as purchasing cough medicine. Congress should understand the point made by Hillary Clinton, who said, "If the FBI is watching you for a suspected terrorist link, you shouldn't be able to just go buy a gun with no questions asked."

CHAPTER 5

FARAAZ AND TARISHI

Islamic terrorists also unleashed an act of terror in Bangladesh on July 1,2016 when Bengali Muslims were getting ready to celebrate Eid at the end of Ramadan. The scope of this terrorist assault was unimaginable, because such atrocities never take place in Bangladesh.

That day terrorists entered the Holey Artisan, a bakery famous for its bagels and coffee, at 8:00 p.m. and opened fire indiscriminately, killing two police officers, Salauddin and Rabiul Islam, who tried to stop them. They immediately took full control of the restaurant by taking hostages, most of whom were foreigners. Throughout the night, some terrorists played a negotiating game with law enforcement while others were busy killing hostages and sending photos of the victims to the IS. The terrorists vowed that this was "only the beginning of the storm" that was intended to punish Prime Minister Sheikh Hasina, who wanted to separate religion from the state by removing from the Bangladesh Constitution Islam's status as the state religion.

Once they realized that the terrorists were negotiating merely to stall for time so that they could kill all the hostages, a commando team from the Bangladesh army stormed the restaurant, ending the 11-hour standoff with the seven terrorists, who killed 22 hostages, including two adolescents: Tarishi Jain, a 19-year-old girl, and Faraaz Hossain, a 20-year-old boy. The tears of the victims' parents joined a wave of anger from not only all corners of Bangladesh but also each and every city worldwide, including New York.

On July 1, I went to NYU with my dad to prepare for my interview with Dr. Lisa Coico, the president of City College of New York. In the basement was a small cafeteria behind the student lounges, in which a large LCD TV monitor hung on the wall. This was where we had watched the horror at the Peshawar School, where terrorists had killed 170 students, including five-year-old Khola. Now, merely a few months later, it seemed I was about to witness another terrorist attack. At 4:00 p.m., as we were passing by the television on our way to buy a Diet Coke, I glanced toward the TV, at CNN, and then turned away quickly.

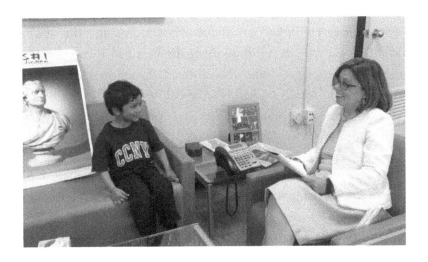

(CCNY President Lisa Coico interviews me).

Faster than words can convey, I thought, *I believe I just saw terrorists killing innocent people in Bangladesh—the country where my dad was born some 40 years ago!* My dad had published some 25 books long before he'd turned 25 years old, and the plots of all these books had been designed to create a secular Bangladesh. However, after writing the poem "Vande Mataram, Bangladesh," he had decided to leave Bangladesh because he'd felt that he had been about to face the same fate as the bloggers who had been killed by Islamic terrorists. I came back to reality when Dad asked me, "Why aren't we solving math problems, Isaac?"

Instead of answering his question, I dragged myself to the nearest sofa and faced the TV screen once more. There, I saw more blood—the blood of children. The seven terrorists had killed almost all the hostages, including Faraaz and Tarishi. Faraaz, a student of Emory University in the US, had gone to Dhaka on his summer vacation and was visiting the café with his Indian friend Tarishi, a student of the University of California at Berkeley. The terrorists started asking Tarishi a series of questions when she failed to recite a verse from the Quran. They then decided to kill her when they learned that she was Hindu. They also killed Faraaz for trying to save a Hindu.

I decided to take to social media, using the hashtag #PrayForBangladesh to unite all Bengalis in a bid to accelerate our anti-IS State campaign. That night, instead of solving math problems, I wrote a speech, which I asked Dad to deliver at NYU. The next day, my dad delivered the speech but was unable to finish it because of an emotional outburst.

Over the next two days, I visited many campuses, where I stood holding a banner that read, "Terrorists have unleashed their terror again. This time, they decided to kill our guests (foreigners) and our angels (children). Now the question is obvious: Why did seven terrorists kill their fellow human beings in the most barbaric way possible?"

The answer is simple: hate. Hate drove them to chant "Allahu Akbar!" while shooting Malala, hate motivated them to shout "Allahu Akbar!" while killing 130 children at a school in Peshawar, hate led two brothers to recite "Allahu Akbar" before killing journalists at the offices of *Charlie Hebdo* in Paris, hate allowed them to kill 137 people in the Paris attack, and hate motivated Omar Mateen to kill 50 people at the Pulse nightclub in Orlando. How can we remove this hate from the minds of people who commit such inhumane acts?

Parents play a major role in instilling hate in the minds of their children, some of whom become terrorists like those who killed many innocent people at the Holey Artisan. True revenge is achieved through education and good moral values only, and to do this, parents should stop giving their children Taliban training and start training them to become scientists like Isaac Newton and Albert Einstein. In addition, they should teach them good moral values so that they may become model citizens for the upcoming Muslim generation. The power of education and moral values is not the best way to take revenge; it is the only way. By doing so, we can make Islam great again. It's time to abandon the illusion and adapt to the reality of Islam.

CHAPTER 6

TERROR AGAINST ROHINGYA

**(On behalf of 400 million Bengalis, New York's
Bangladesh Press Club and Time Television gave me a
huge reception in Jackson Heights, New York, in honor
of the recognition I received from President Obama)**

On December 10, 1929, at Calcutta's Albert Hall, Bengalis threw a grand reception for Kazi Nazrul Islam, their most illustrious son. Some 88 years later, on January 13, 2017, Bengalis gave me a similar reception. On behalf of 400 million Bengalis, New York's Bangladesh Press Club and Time Television gave me a huge reception in Jackson Heights, New York, in honor of the recognition I received from President Barack Obama for being able to solve PhD-level math, physics, and chemistry problems at only four years old.

(On behalf of the reception community, Sibli Chowdhury Kayes, Secretary of New York Bangladesh Press Club, escorted me to the stage to give a speech).

Millions of people around the world also watched Time Television, which broadcasted the reception live on its website. I was invited to give a speech at the event. The following is what I said:

Assalamualaikum.

My name is Soborno Isaac Bari. I'm a five-year-old, and I consider Rohingya my own family.

President Obama said that he was very proud of me because I could solve PhD-level math, physics, and chemistry problems. Harvard University gave me recognition for my contribution to math and science. So, I should be solving math problems now, rather than giving a speech. But the faces of many lifeless children of Rohingya, such as my brother Abdul Masood, forced me to make this speech. How can I solve math problems when Aung San Suu Kyi refused to stop killing my Rohingya family? Today, I came here as a brother of Abdul Masood, a 40-day-old boy who lost his life due to the reckless behavior of Myanmar leader, Aung San Suu Kyi. I came here to give this speech for the dignity of Masood. I came here to give this speech for the dignity of all Rohingyas. I came here to give this speech for the dignity of all Muslims. I came here to give this speech for the dignity of all human beings.

Rohingyas started living in Burma in 3000 BC. But thousands of years later, my Rohingya family is still not free. Thousands of years later, Rohingya still has not gained voting power. Thousands of years later, Rohingya still has no access to education. Thousands of years later, my Rohingya family still finds itself in exile in its own country. Thousands of years later, Rohingyas are still homeless. Thousands of years later, Rohingya husbands are still forced to watch their wives being raped by Buddhist monks. Thousands of years later, Rohingya parents still find the dead bodies of their children floating in the water. This is why I came here to give this speech—to stop this evil. This is why I want you to stand up against this evil.

(Giving a historic speech in front of thousands of people)

We shouldn't call this crisis in Burma a Rohingya problem. We shouldn't call it a Muslim problem. We should call it a human problem. In fact, we should call it a human crisis, because when Aung San Suu Kyi, a Nobel Laureate, is responsible for the death of a 40-day-old boy, Abdul Masood, then you just can't call it a Rohingya problem; you call it a human crisis. When Aung San Suu Kyi, a woman, is responsible for the rape of thousands of Rohingya women, then you don't call it a Muslim problem; you call it a human problem. In fact, you don't call it a human problem; you call it a human tragedy. When Aung San Suu Kyi, the prime minister (also known as the leader) of Myanmar, is responsible for the deaths of thousands of Rohingyas, you just want to scream to save humanity from this lady Hitler. This is why I'm giving this speech to correct her behavior. This is why I want you to stand up to save the millions of victims like Abdul Masood from Aung San Suu Kyi. This is why I want you to stand up and step up with me to save my Rohingya family from Aung San Suu Kyi.

HARVARD UNIVERSITY

OFFICE OF THE PRESIDENT
(617) 495-1502

MASSACHUSETTS HALL
CAMBRIDGE, MASSACHUSETTS 02138

May 2, 2018

Mr. Soborno Isaac Bari
80 Strong Street, Apt. 5F
Bronx, NY 10468

Dear Soborno,

It is a pleasure to write on the very special occasion of your sixth birthday. I hope that the year ahead is filled with many wonderful learning experiences and joy, and I wish you all the best for your future.

Sincerely,

Drew Gilpin Faust

Now, I want to talk to 1.7 billion Muslims as directly as possible as a brother. Listen to me: nothing is more important than education. President Obama gave me recognition because of my love for education. Oxford University Vice Chancellor, Dr. Richardson, sent me a gift because I love math and science. City College of New York president, Lisa Coico, called me the "Einstein of our time" because of my commitment to secular education. Unfortunately, the children of Rohingyas are mostly uneducated. This is because they don't have access to school, because their bodies are weak from hunger, because their sickness goes unnoticed, and because their lives are spent in hopeless poverty. I want every Rohingya child to at least dream of becoming the next Isaac Newton or Albert Einstein. In order to do so, these children need to have a philosophy, which my father calls the Rohingya philosophy.

In his article, Justice for Rohingya, my father wrote that the Rohingya philosophy is a self-help philosophy that includes sending all Rohingya children to school, making them fall in love with math and science, reading books, and having a maximum of two children per family. The core of the Rohingya philosophy is this: plant a dream in the minds of all Rohingya children that they, too, can become the next Isaac Newton and Albert Einstein.

THE WHITE HOUSE
WASHINGTON

November 2, 2016

Soborno Bari
Bronx, New York

Dear Soborno:

I hope you take pride in all your hard work and accomplishments.

America needs students like you who are trying hard in school, dreaming big dreams, and improving our communities. Our country faces many challenges, but we will overcome them if we join together in common purpose. I encourage you to continue to put your best effort into everything you do, and I want you to know I expect great things from you.

Young people like you are tomorrow's leaders—you inspire me and give me tremendous hope for the future. Michelle and I wish you all the best.

Sincerely,

I have a dream that Aung San Suu Kyi will soon join me in promoting the Rohingya philosophy. I have a dream that Aung San Suu Kyi will soon visit Bangladesh to bring all Rohingyas back to Burma. I have a dream that Aung San Suu Kyi will soon invite me to Burma to visit my Rohingya family, especially the family of my brother, Abdul Masood. I have a dream that Aung San Suu Kyi will soon wake up and live out the true meaning of her father's dream. Buddhist monks and Rohingyas are two branches of the same tree. This is the tree of Myanmar. I have a dream that one day, in the Burmese Parliament, the sons of Rohingyas and the sons of Buddhist monks will sit down together at the table of brotherhood to collaborate with Aung San Suu Kyi on how to build a modern Myanmar. I have a dream that one day, Aung San Suu Kyi will hold a Rohingya baby and give him or her a kiss on the cheek. I have a dream that one day, Aung San Suu Kyi will meet the parents of every single child of the Rohingya genocide, such as the parents of 40-day-old Abdul Masood, and apologize for her terror. This is the only way that the departed soul of my brother, Abdul Masood, will forgive Aung San Suu Kyi. This is the only way that she can achieve a united Myanmar. Thank you.

CHAPTER 7

TWO BROTHERS

It was July 3, 2017, and we remembered what had happened the previous year. We still remembered how the imam refused to pray for America and how I ran to George Washington's statue to apologize on behalf of the imam for refusing to pray for America. The only difference was that it wasn't Eid, and I wasn't going to the mosque with my father. Instead, my elder brother, Albert, and I were about to go to school alone, as we always did, and as always, my mother wished us a farewell. Albert went to Brooklyn Tech. I found myself alone in the middle of the road, thinking about my upcoming interview with MIT scientist Dr. Daniel Kabat. However, as I was walking to school, I saw an American flag stuck under the tires of a black Honda. Its stars were bruised, and the flag pole seemed about to break under the pressure of the tires. I was deeply disturbed, believing that this was an insult to the American flag. After many attempts, I was still unable to nudge the flag out from under the tire. I decided to wait until the driver came to move the car so that I could save the American flag from being disrespected. Time passed, and it was almost 4 p.m. As Albert was returning from Brooklyn Tech, he saw a boy, who looked like his brother, sitting on a piece of chopped wood next to a black Honda. Albert ran toward me and saw that it really was me.

(Promoting math and science during Namaj to help youth understand this: there is something more important than religion and that is solving more and more math problems).

Bewildered, he observed for a few minutes, trying to process the situation. He then yelled, "Isaac! What are you doing here?"

I replied nervously, "Albert, I didn't go to school."

"Didn't go to school?! Why?"

(Kathleen Raab thanked Isaac for changing her perception of Muslims. When Isaac asked why she wanted to take a picture

with him even though he wasn't a celebrity, Katy responded, "You might not be a celebrity, but you are a hero for people like me, whose whole view of the world has changed because of you.")

Pointing to the flag, I said, "I was trying to pull it out, but I couldn't. So, I was waiting for the driver to come and move the car so that I could stop the flag from being disrespected and bruised."

This made Albert so emotional that his eyes filled with tears. He cried out, "Are you OK, my little brother?"

"Albert, don't tell Mom and Dad, please."

"OK, Isaac. I won't tell them. But what I *will* tell them is that you are on a mission to change the world." Soon thereafter, Albert helped push the car, and I was able to stop the flag from being disrespected.

After I got home that day, I asked Dad to take me to George Washington's statue in Union Square so that I could read the first US president his apology on behalf of 1.7 billion Muslims. As I began reading my letter—"Dear Founding Father, I came here to say sorry"—several dozen people lined up behind me, hoping to take a few pictures with me. As the people dispersed, I noticed that one of the ones remaining was Kathleen Raab, who thanked me for changing her perception of Muslims. When I asked why she wanted to take a picture with me even though I wasn't a celebrity, she responded, "You might not be a celebrity, but you are a hero for people like me, whose whole view of the world has changed because of you."

Next day, another unforgettable event unfolded. As I walked through Times Square with Dad on Independence Day, he saw a guitarist performing on the street. Just a few seconds prior, Dad and I had been discussing some math problems, but I immediately stopped: "Dad, I need to go tell that man that he is singing the wrong song. It is the Fourth of July, and singing anything but "The Star-Spangled Banner" is not only disrespectful but also an insult to this great nation we live in." After he gave me permission, I ran to the man, Lawrence Rush, and shouted, "Stop the music!" Soon thereafter, he began singing "The Star-Spangled Banner," and many other people joined in with me to spread the patriotism.

(Upon getting off the train, Soborno saw a singer, Lawrence Rush, singing a pop song. Soborno ran to him and shouted, "Stop the music!" Soon thereafter, they

began singing "The Star-Spangled Banner," and they later moved around the city to spread the patriotism.)

This series of events convinced my dad to make the documentary *I'm Muslim & I love America*. He wanted to tell people this story so that they would be inspired by me. But Dad faced a dilemma: he was neither a writer nor a director, and he didn't even have the necessary equipment. And I am a math and science whiz, not a movie star. I received recognition from Harvard University for being able to solve PhD-level math, physics, and chemistry problems, not for acting.

A few days later, my dad and I met with Kathleen Raab and Lawrence Rush and asked them to act in the documentary, because my dad wanted to tell this story to the world. What he did not tell them is that he didn't even own a camera. All he had was a broken and dysfunctional iPhone that he'd dropped many times. I'm not even sure whether it's still capable of recording. In fact, most of the time, the shooting of the movie was done using Katy's or Lawrence's iPhone.

Later we went to the BCC to pay tribute to the founding father. There, we met a photographer, who took my picture for the newspaper. He asked me, "Why did you make this movie?"

I replied, "I made this movie to show that we don't need more imams. We need more Al-Khawarizmis, not imams."

On the way back home, Dad asked me, "Why don't you do something for Bangladesh? You always do things for America."

I responded, "If I change Bangladesh, I change only Bangladesh. But if I change America, I change the world."

The day begins with Soborno Isaac, a five-year-old Muslim boy who brings home a Christmas tree to celebrate the birth of Jesus Christ on December 25. However, there is a problem. His mother, a devout Muslim, does not like the idea. The conflict between mother and son begins to heat up.

CHAPTER 8

MOTHER VS. SON

There is a saying that time flies. I had already turned five and was ready to bring home a Christmas tree to celebrate the birth of Jesus Christ on December 25. However, there was a problem: my mother, a devout Muslim, did not like the idea. The conflict between mother and son began heating up.

Isaac: Why can't a Muslim celebrate Christmas, Mom?

Mom: I don't know, and I don't need to know. All I know is I'm a Muslim, and Muslims don't celebrate Christmas.

Isaac: I'm also a Muslim, Mom, and I love my religion. However, I'm also a Hindu, a Buddha, a Jew, and a Christian. I know we love Eid, but we should also love Yom Kippur, Saraswati, Buddha

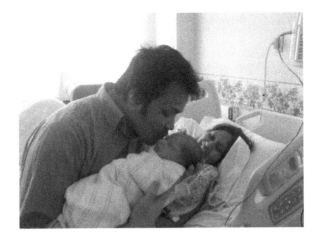

(I was born on April 9, 2012 at New York Hospital Queens now known as NewYork-Presbyterian Queens)

Purnima, and Christmas. We should love all religions, and I think we should celebrate every holiday as our own.

However, my mother's 40-year-old traditional mind was unwilling to accept the reasoning of my five-year-old mind. As a result, she threw the Christmas tree into a garbage truck. I became enraged and left home, announcing that I would not return until I found my Christmas tree. On my way out, I wrote a very emotional letter to my mom:

Dear Mom,

I love you, but I did not like you throwing out my Christmas tree. I know you are a Muslim; I'm a Muslim, too. However, I'm not only a Muslim but also a Hindu, a Buddha, a Jew, and a Christian. I love Eid, but I also love Saraswati, Magha Puja, Yom Kippur, and Christmas.

I love all holidays because whichever human products we can enjoy, including Eid and Christmas, should instantly become ours, regardless of their origin. As a Muslim, I am proud of my humanity when I can acknowledge the festivals of other religions as my own. We should all feel gratitude that every great holiday, including Christmas, is ours.

I know you are praying for me to find my Christmas tree. I love you, Mom.

Yours,

Soborno Isaac

Coincidentally, Lawrence Rush and Kathleen Raab would soon join me in searching for my Christmas tree.

Meanwhile, my mom realized her mistake, and she made a banner on which she quoted my words: "I'm a Muslim, but I'm also a Hindu, a Buddha, a Jew, and a Christian. I love Eid, Durga Puja, Buddha Purnima, Hanukkah, and Christmas. I belong to all religions, and every great holiday is mine, including Eid and Christmas." She went to every single mall, holding up her banner in hopes of finding me.

Lawrence and I tried our best to find the Christmas tree, but we couldn't find it. Lawrence gave up, but I refused to give up and go home without my tree. It was Christmas Eve, and I was sitting in Central Park reading aloud my letter to my mom. As the people dispersed, one of those remaining was Kathleen Raab.

She asked me, "What are you doing here, Isaac? It's a very cold day!" I explained my story and sought her help. We became friends instantly, and she offered her help. We hired a horse-drawn carriage to take us all around the city in hopes of finding my Christmas tree. We found the tree in Central Park.

My mother apologized to me and decided to celebrate Christmas, and we have been celebrating Christmas ever since. This message of love has spread around the world, including to Bangladesh, where physics teacher Nahid Afzal, his son Faiyaz, and their friend Noman Lam decided to promote my philosophy. They made 68,000 posters for the 68,000 villages of Bangladesh. The posters stated in Bangla, "I'm a Muslim, but I'm also a Hindu, a Buddha, a Jew, and a Christian. I love Eid, Durga Puja, Buddha Purnima, Hanukkah, and Christmas. I belong to all religions, and every holiday, including Eid and Christmas, is mine."

This series of events convinced my dad to make another documentary: *I'm Muslim and I love Christmas.* This time, it was directed by a well-known director named Uday Bengali. He wanted to share this story, especially with the 1.7 billion Muslims worldwide so that they, too, could be inspired by it.

I am a fan of Kazi Nazrul Islam, the poet Laureate of Bangladesh, who expressed his vision of religious harmony in an editorial in *Joog Bani* in 1920: "Come, Brother Hindu! Come, Musalman! Come, Buddhist! Come, Christian! Let us transcend all barriers; let us forsake forever all smallness, all lies, and all selfishness; and let us call brothers as brothers. We shall quarrel no more . . ."

PHOTO ALBUM:

Zahid Hossain, a poor man who occasionally pulled rickshaws to earn money, published a book on Soborno

Kadir Chowdhury Babul founded the Soborno Isaac Math & Science Lab in Sylhet to inspire young people to focus on math and science instead of terrorism

Soborno Isaac's movie, *I'm Muslim & I love America*, inspired millions of children in Bangladesh, such as five-year-old Dihan, to rise against terrorism.

Joy Kumar Roy, a Hindu and a fan of Soborno Isaac, promoting his message in Shariatpur (শরিয়তপুর), to create a world without terrorism.

Md Abdur Rahman promoted Soborno's message in Comilla (কুমিল্লা) to create a world without terrorism. He was inspired by Soborno's movie and motivated to promote his message that we are all Muslim, but "we love all other religions, including Hinduism, Buddhism, Christianity, and Judaism. We celebrate Eid, but we also love celebrating Christmas and other holidays."

Even the faculty members at various universities in Bangladesh, including Professor Paul Tapan Kumar, joined the revolution.

On behalf of all Muslim students at JU, <u>Asad Uz Zaman</u> joined Soborno Isaac to create a world without terrorism.

On behalf of all Muslim students at Lalbagh Model School & College, Mehrab Hasan Taaz and his friends joined Soborno to create a world without terrorism.

Professor Mirza Nahid Hossain involved his children in the revolution to inspire other youth to step up. Thanking Ryan, Soborno wrote, "Thank you for sending me your son Rayan's poster. In fact, this is not a poster; this is the revolution, which I called "The Love".

Inspired by Soborno's movie, Anisul Islam has led the University of Chittagong in the revolution against terrorism.

Dear Mr. Asrar Habib Nipu, I'm so proud of your son Jarif: this poster has what it takes to accelerate my campaign "The ❣," which aims to create a world without terrorism. Jarif not only sent a poster for me, but he also sent a piece of Bangladesh along with it.

"Dear <u>Ezaz</u> This poster will go down in history as an agent of change, and it will inspire my family, "The ❣," to create a world without terrorism.

Hello, world. In case you didn't know (him), this "Bepul" is the Bepul of Barisal University. More specifically, he is the Bepul of Bangladesh. His poster helped me discover that Bangladesh will lead the next revolution of the world under my leadership and that its aim is to create a world without terrorism

BRAC University joined the revolution against terrorism.

On behalf of all students of the ✋ Bangladesh Navy School & College, <u>Ashikul Islam Emon</u> joined me to create a world without terrorism through the book and movie *The Love*.

"When a specific university goes low, Jahangirnagar University goes high against terrorism. Stand up with me. It's time to Salute JU." On behalf of all students of Jahangirnagar University, <u>Sazid Hossain</u> joined me to create a world without terrorism through the book and movie *The Love*.

I have never seen perfection, but I have seen <u>Rabiul Awal Sizan</u>. Every time I see this poster, it brings tears to my eyes. Thank you, Sizan, for joining me to create a world without terrorism.

Dear <u>Shihab</u>, When I looked at your poster, I screamed: <u>Soborno</u> unleash *The Love* to create a world without terrorism by planting a dream in the mind of every child that he or she can be the next Sir Isaac Newton and Albert Einstein.

Soborno's message of love has spread around the world, including to Bangladesh, where a teacher, Safir, and his son decided to promote Isaac's philosophy by creating 68,000 posters for 68,000 villages in Bangladesh.

Inspired by Isaac's movie, Rayhan Himu has led Dhaka University in the revolution against terrorism.

In hopes of creating a world without terrorism, fans of Soborno Isaac posted 68,000 posters in 68,000 villages in Bangladesh

On behalf of Daffodil International University, Rifat Hossain joined Soborno Isaac to create a world without terrorism.

Upon getting off the train, Soborno saw a singer, Lawrence Rush, singing a pop song. Soborno ran to him and shouted, "Stop the music!" Soon thereafter, they began singing "The Star-Spangled Banner," and they later moved around the city to spread the patriotism.

Dear <u>Afrin Dina,</u> Thank you for sending a historic poster for my campaign, which aims to create a world without terrorism through the support of *The Love* family. In fact, I am honored to have received your poster, because when a Muslim woman stands up against terrorism, the whole world starts respecting Islam and its followers, Muslims. Once again, thanks, Afrin, for taking the initiative to restore the dignity of Islam by rising against terrorism.

Zahid Hossain, my biographer, walked over 100 miles around Bangladesh, holding Sadiyan's banner to promote women's support for my anti-terrorism campaign.

Tarika Akter Shathe rose up against terror to accelerate my efforts to create a world without terrorism. Stand up and salute Shathe.

The poster held by Jerin Tasnim, a student of KU, is not actually a poster; rather, it's a manifesto aimed at creating a world without terrorism.

A historic day for Bangladesh and for the Muslim world. It's also a historic moment for Jahangirnagar University (✋): when a so-called university goes low, Jahangirnagar University goes high against terrorism, thanks to <u>Sinthia Silvi.</u>

On behalf of all crew members of I Love Christmas, Uday Bangali, who graduated from the University of Dhaka, joined Soborno Isaac to create a world without terrorism. Here's what Isaac wrote in his notebook today: "One day, I'll be on the stage receiving an Oscar, along with Uday, HrishiKesh, and Safir, for promoting my campaign through your movie."

Three fans of Soborno Safir and his son, along with their friend, decided to promote Isaac's philosophy in Bangladesh. They made 68,000 posters for the 68,000 villages in Bangladesh. The posters stated in Bangla, "I'm a Muslim, but I'm also a Hindu, a Buddhist, a Jew, and a Christian. I love Eid, Durga Puja, Buddha Purnima, Hanukkah, and Christmas. I belong to all religions, and every holiday, including Eid and Christmas, is mine."

On behalf of all Muslims who live in France, <u>Abdullah Al Mamun Khan</u> joined Soborno Isaac to create a world without terrorism.

On behalf of all Muslims who live in India, Hasan joined Soborno Isaac to create a world without terrorism.

kazi Alfu joined Soborno Isaac to create a world without terrorism.

On behalf of all Muslims who live in England, Sarker Mohiuddin Hasnat Lenin joined Soborno Isaac to create a world without terrorism.

CHAPTER 9

A WORLD WITHOUT TERRORISM

As the world moves forward, with women going to school, men critiquing the government, and philosophers contemplating, the Muslim world, especially the Middle East, is taking steps backward, with men ensuring that they maintain their lofty positions (e.g., not allowing women to drive and the right to keep four wives at the same time) and that women remain busy adding more pieces to their burkas. Naturally, we inquire into who is responsible for such backwardness, and, of course, the answer we receive is no surprise—the terrorist organizations, especially the Taliban and IS.

I am familiar with all kinds of terrorism as a result of watching terrorist acts over and over on TV, the first being on December 16; then, in Washington, D.C.; then, at Lehman College; and finally, back at the NYU Bobst Library. I've also read stories of Hitler and his terrorism. The Nazis killed more than two-thirds of the Jewish population of Europe. What made the Nazis barbaric was that they did not hesitate to kill, even if the victim was a child. What makes Islamic terrorists worse than Nazis is that jihadists are not only happy to kill but also happy to commit suicide (e.g., the hijackers in the 9/11 attacks).

The Nazis were one-dimensional animals. Their mission was to promptly kill all the Jews. The jihadists, however, are two-dimensional animals. Their mission is to kill others and kill themselves. They kidnap innocent people and sometimes burn them alive or behead them before the cameras. They also proudly display the dead victims' heads and bodies, releasing the still or video images via the Internet. If they are unable to kidnap their victims, they unleash the suicide bombers.

I must admit that there were moments when I would read about jihadists' horrific acts in the newspaper and force myself to shut my eyes, keeping them closed to hide my tears. As a well-read person, I am familiar with the carnage that helped IS spread terror from Iraq to Yemen, including the beheadings of James Foley, Steven Sotloff, David Haines, Alan Henning, and Kenji Goto, as well as the burning alive of Jordanian pilot Moaz Kassasbeh. I am familiar with the cruel disregard for human life and the heinous religious ideologies that motivated jihadists to play a part in the deaths of hundreds of Syrian, Kurdish, and Afghan soldiers. Reading about these tragedies, I just wanted to scream, "The Middle East used to mean the cradle of civilization!" However, today it means *kidnap, behead, and broadcast.* It means "I'm about to kidnap non-Muslims and behead them."

It means "I'm about to mix the victims' blood with the seawater." It means "I'm about to kidnap a pilot and burn him alive." It means "I'm about to detonate a bomb inside a crowded mosque." It means "I'm about to destroy prehistoric statues and artifacts."

It means "If I'm from the Middle East, then I'm a terrorist."

Despite my familiarity with their barbarism, little can prepare a poor reader such as me to hear the grisly accounts of the mass beheadings of 21 Egyptian Christians.

IS first reported the mass kidnapping of Egyptian Christians in its newspaper, *Dabiq*. The report included pictures of all 21 captives, including two brothers, Bishoy Kamel, 25, and Samuel Kamel, 22. Both brothers earned university degrees but had to migrate to Libya in search of work because they were unable to find jobs in their home country. They actually planned to return to Egypt when they heard about the IS presence in the Libyan city, but it was too late. IS kidnapped them along, with 19 others, and threatened to kill them to avenge the killing of Osama bin Laden. Eventually, the IS terrorists took them to the Mediterranean coast on February 5, 2015, where they beheaded them, along with the other 19 captives. "The sea in which you've hidden Sheikh Osama bin Laden's body," said one jihadist before the beheading of the Kamel brothers, "we swear to Allah we will mix it with your blood."

(Channel i sent its senior journalist, Mustafa Mollick, to come to the United States to take Soborno Isaac interview. Millions watch it on TV. Recently, Mustafa wrote a book on Soborno).

These are stories that are usually found within the realms of horror movies. One brother was forced to watch the beheading of the other and to watch as men took their revenge by mixing the blood of the captives with the seawater. The mass murder of the 21 Egyptian Christians was, indeed, unprecedented in its horror. No other terrorist event involved such rapid, targeted, and deliberate brutality, nor was any other so tightly bound to the idea that people had to be beheaded and their blood mixed with the seawater. When I read this in the newspaper, I cried out loud, and tears trickled from my disbelieving eyes. I said, "Jihadists of the Islamic State, you are not Muslims. You are monsters. You are disgusting bastards."

Unfortunately, these disgusting bastards are gaining momentum in the southern part of the Middle East and especially in Yemen, where they possess a stronghold similar to the ones they already have in Iraq, Syria, and Libya. In fact, IS unleashed its suicide bombers on crowded mosques in Yemen, killing over 140 worshipers, all of whom were Muslims.

These stories would make any rational thinker question why terrorists of the IS group, who claim to be Muslims, hiding bombs on their bodies to kill Muslims worshiping in mosques? Even Nazis did not kill Nazis, nor did the Khmer Rouge kill the Khmer Rouge; yet, Muslims kill Muslims all the time.

When I read these kinds of stories in the newspaper, I ask myself, *What motivates these men to kill and commit suicide?* The answer is religion. In fact, terrorists used Islam to reestablish the caliphate, which is the concept of a one-world government system led by successors of the Prophet Muhammad. I read the Quran with my mother to find my own answers. I read in the Holy Book that "If you kill one person, it is as if you kill the whole humanity." We have to stop terrorists from misinterpreting the Quran. However, educational and socioeconomic solutions are much more elusive than religious solutions. The separation of the church and state has worked for so many countries, including America.

So, it should work for the Middle East, too.

CHAPTER 10

PRESIDENT ISEKENEGBE AND THE INTRODUCTION OF THIS BOOK

I received a letter from Dr. Thomas Isekenegbe, the president of Bronx C. College, inviting me to be interviewed. This was nothing new to me. In fact, I had gotten used to giving interviews to presidents and scientists at various American universities since I had turned two years old.

(MIT Professor Mizanul Chowdhury, who writes codes for NASA International Space Station, interviews me at FOBANA, in front of thousands of people including Congresswoman Barbara Comstack).

I remember giving my first interview to Vice President Jerald Posman at Medgar Evers College in 2014. In 2015, Dr. Lisa Coico, President of City College of New York, interviewed me for three hours. In 2016, I was interviewed by Lehman College president, Ricardo Fernandez. In 2017, Dr. Daniel Kabat, an MIT scientist, interviewed me on topics ranging from light to black holes. Similar to previous years, I had received many interview requests in 2018, and I decided to sit down with President Isekenegbe.

(Dr. Brian Murphy, chair of Math & Computer Science at Lehman College, interviews me)

Toward the end of the interview, which focused on calculus and chemistry, Dr. Isekenegbe suddenly switched gears. "What do you do in your free time?"

"I'm working on a book called *The Love*."

"*The Love*?"

"Yes. It's a story about a Muslim child's struggle to create a world without terrorism."

"Who is that Muslim child?"

"Me."

"Why did you decide to write a book at such an early age?"

"I had no plan. But one day, when I was praying at a mosque, I asked the imam to pray for America because it was the Eve of Fourth of July, but the imam refused to pray. This is why I came to your college to stand in front of the George Washington statue and say sorry on behalf of the imam. A Bronx C. College journalist interviewed me. Meanwhile, I received a letter from President Obama, but I decided to meet with him after I changed every imam's behavior. My mission was simple—to inspire them to fall in love with America through my documentary, I'm Muslim and *I Love Christmas*."

(President Isekenegbe interviews me).

"*I love Christmas*? But I thought you were Muslim."

"I lost my periodic table when I was two years old, and I found it with the help of Santa Claus. Ever since then, I've celebrated Christmas, but my mom said that as a Muslim, I shouldn't celebrate any other religious festivals. So, I decided to inspire my mom and every member of my family to fall in love with every religion in the world. A Bengali film maker, Udoy, made a documentary to promote my philosophy in Bangladesh. He named the movie, *I Love Christmas*."

"You know, I'm a Christian, but I come from a family that has many Muslim members. So, tell me more about your book."

(MIT Scientist Dr. Daniel Kabat interviews me).

"I divided the book into ten chapters, and the first few are based on my experience with terrorism. For example, I was exposed to the horror of terror at the NYU library for the first time when I was two years old. I went there to solve some math problems with my dad but ended up watching the Taliban kill nearly 200 schoolchildren at the Peshawar School."

"What is the main philosophy of *The Love*?"

"As a Muslim, I love Islam. But I also love Hinduism, Buddhism, Judaism, and Christianity. I love to celebrate Eid. But I also love to celebrate Durga Puja, Modhu Purnima, Rosh Hashanah, and Christmas. Let's unleash love to create a world without terrorism."

"Thank you, Isaac, for helping me understand the main philosophy of your book, *The Love.* Hopefully, this will inspire Bronx Community College students, as well as the Bronx College community, to fall in love with every single religion."

"Why don't you write the introduction of this book?"

"I will."

CHAPTER 11

DREAMS FROM MY FATHER

My father is a math professor at Bronx C. College. However, many people don't know that he worked as a security guard for 15 years (2000–2015). So, how can someone with such an unconventional past end up becoming a university faculty member who works every day to inspire hundreds of students to fall in love with mathematics? How can a security guard end up getting into a doctoral program at Columbia University?

It all began when my dad moved to America from Bangladesh in 2000. After four years of studies, he earned a GED in 2004, and that same year, he commenced postsecondary studies at the Borough of Manhattan Community College. Over the last 13 years, he has earned five bachelor's degrees—BAs in political science, economics, mathematics, physics, and computer science—from York College, Brooklyn College, and Lehman College, respectively. He has also earned two master's degrees: an MA in Political Science from Brooklyn College and an MA in Physics Education from NYU. He wants to earn three more doctoral degrees in three additional subjects (physics, chemistry, and computer science) before he runs for governor of New York. His ultimate goal is to create a world without terrorism by planting a dream in the mind of every child that he or she can become the next Sir Isaac Newton or Albert Einstein. To do so, my dad launched an anti-terrorism campaign called the Bari Science Lab. But ISIS didn't like it, and back in 2014 and 2015, they threatened my dad to terminate his campaign on social media. Instead of terminating the campaign, my dad involved my brother and me, but our family isn't strong enough to defeat terrorism alone. We need support, especially from the US government.

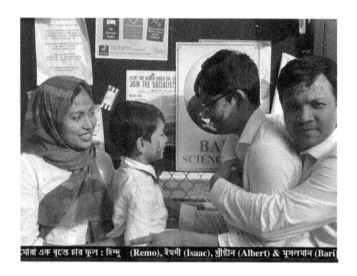

মারা এক বৃত্তে চার ফুল : হিন্দু (Remo), ইহুদী (Isaac), খ্রীষ্টান (Albert) & মুসলমান (Bari)

(My home is the hub of religious tolerance: We're celebrating Nazrul birthday. Nazrul received intense criticism from religious Muslims for his assimilation of Hindu philosophy and culture with Islam in his works and for openly denouncing many Islamic teachings. Although a Muslim, he gave his sons both Hindu and Muslim names: Krishna Mohammad, Arindam Khaled (Bulbul), Kazi Sabhyasachi and Kazi Aniruddha)

The US also needs to bear in mind that these terrorist organizations (including ISIS) are not isolated cults; rather, they comprise a culture that feels empathy for Osama bin Laden. It should be noted that most Arabs, especially those of the older generation, are illiterate. (For them, literacy means reading the verses of the Koran.) It's easy for ISIS terrorists to control the minds of these illiterate people.

However, this challenge can be overcome by establishing a

socioeconomic revolution via education. Let's unleash education to correct the behavior of the Taliban, and let's start this process at NYU. In fact, many of my dad's professors at NYU joined us in this endeavor, including Professor Blonstein, who wrote, "We share your outrage at the actions of those who slaughtered children in Peshawar School in the name of something they believe in."

My dad promptly responded to Professor Blonstein's letter: "More than 100 years ago, Ralph Waldo Emerson said that a foolish inevitability is the hobgoblin of little minds."

When one becomes enamored with a principle, as the Taliban has done, one also becomes blind to its alternatives. As such, it is as though a hobgoblin has entered one's imagination and blocks both new ideas and the ability to see different perspectives. To address this, we need to analyze a deeper question: who is actually insulting Islam? I will examine this in the next chapter, titled "Let's Fall in Love with Math and Science."

When I asked my dad, he replied with his own question, "When do the lives of 15 million people have a greater value than 1.3 billion?" Upon hearing such a quantitative answer, I was clueless. Dad added, "Well, if 1.3 billion people suddenly disappear, the world will not be affected that much. However, if 15 million people vanished, the world would suffer very much." It took me a few hours to understand his analogy.

My dad actually made a comparison between the total number of Muslims and Jews. The total number of Muslims is about 1.8 billion, and the total number of Jews is about 15 million. The total population of the earth at present is 7. 5billion. Among these, 2.2 billion are Christian, 1.8 billion are followers of Islam, and there are only 15 million Jewish believers. More precisely, I would say that 24% of the world's total population is Muslim, while only 0.2% is Jewish. In every kind of mathematical problem, a value of 24% is more than 0.2%. So, the world would be in catastrophic crisis if 24% of its population suddenly disappeared, as opposed to 0.2%. After thinking about this, I wondered the point that my dad was trying to make. This reminded me of the famous Muslim Nobel Laureate Abdus Salam.

In 1980, Salam published his book, *Gauge Unification Fundamental Forces*, a modest proposal to empower Muslims to reenter the world of math, science, and technology before they became completely marginalized. The grave humor of his extreme proposal was to remind Muslims about the consequences of neglecting education and focusing too much on religion, including hatred toward Christian and Jews. Dad's quantitative analysis of Muslims' violence against innocent people was so fantastic that, at first, I thought it was satire in the tradition of Salam. Let's look at this analogy in detail.

Until now, a total of 900 people have won the Nobel Prize. Among them, the number of Jewish people is 203 (23 %), and the number of Muslims is 10. According to my math, 1 out of 23 laureates should have been Muslims. If this were so, among the 900 laureates, Muslims should have received at least 170 Nobel Prizes. However, the reality is not even close to these expectations. Muslims neither attained 170 nor 17; they won only 10 Nobel Prizes! Contrastingly, as per the numbers I calculated that were representative of the population, Jewish believers should not have attained more than three or four Nobel Prizes; yet, they received more than 203. Upon realizing this fact, I instantly understood my dad's analogy and was filled with shame and guilt as a Muslim. The question is obvious: what are Muslims doing?

"I don't think these are Muslims; these are the Peter Pans of Islam: the little children who refused to grow up," said Dr. Daniel Kabat, the MIT scientist with whom I am investigating black holes.

The Muslims who kill others in many terrorist attacks, including 9/11, are completely wrong, because killing is not the way to achieve revenge. For real retribution, produce Isaac Newtons and Albert

Einsteins in every home. Instead of killing innocent people, send a man to the moon, build schools like Oxford and Harvard in every city, invest in research to find an AIDS vaccine, or win more Nobel Prizes every year.

If you think it's impossible to achieve success as a Muslim in America, just look at my father. If he can become a professor after working as a security guard for 15 years, so can you.

Kathleen Raab thanked Isaac for changing her perception of Muslims. When Isaac asked why she wanted to take a picture with him even though he wasn't a celebrity, Katy responded, "You might not be a celebrity, but you are a hero for people like me, whose whole view of the world has changed because of you."

BIO

Soborno Isaac Bari is a six-year-old student enrolled in gifted and talented program in New York City. In 2014, Dr. Lisa Coico, president of City College of New York, gave him the title "Einstein of our time." In 2016, President Obama gave him recognition for being able to solve advanced math, physics, chemistry, and computer science problems. Sir John Bercow, Speaker of British Parliament, wrote, "I would like to congratulate Soborno Isaac for his remarkable academic achievements which have come to the attention of such luminaries as President Obama and Dr. Lisa Coico, amongst others." On May 2, 2018, Soborno Isaac received recognition from Dr. Drew Gilpin Faust, the president of Harvard University. Soborno Isaac is currently working on two projects: he is creating Nazrul, which is a humanoid robot, and collaborating with Dr. Daniel Kabat, an MIT (The Massachusetts Institute of Technology) scientist, on a new book titled *The Black Holes*.

CPSIA information can be obtained
at www.ICGtesting.com
Printed in the USA
FSHW010503150621
82392FS